AF438921

Elspeth and the Visitor

I Talk You Talk Press

Copyright © 2021 I Talk You Talk Press

ISBN: 978-4-909733-67-2

www.italkyoutalk.com

info@italkyoutalk.com

All rights reserved. No part of this publication may be resold, reproduced, stored in retrieval system, copied in any form or by any means, electronic, mechanical, photocopying, recording or otherwise transmitted without the prior written permission from the publisher. You must not circulate this publication in any format, online or otherwise.

This is a work of fiction. Names, characters, businesses, organizations, products, places, events and incidents are either the products of the author's imagination or are used in a fictitious manner. We have no affiliation with any existing companies mentioned in this story. Any resemblance to actual persons, living or dead, existing stories or actual events is purely coincidental.

Although the author and publisher have made every effort to ensure that the contents of this book were correct at press time, the author and publisher do not assume and hereby disclaim any liability to any party for any loss, damage, or disruption caused by errors or omissions, whether such errors or omissions result from negligence, accident, or any other cause.

For more information, see the Copyright Notice on our website.

The cover illustration contains an image from Adobe for which we have purchased the appropriate license.
Image copyright: © ysbrandcosijn #316398482 Standard License

CONTENTS

I Talk You Talk Press

CHAPTER ONE

Elspeth was cleaning the house. It was a beautiful sunny day, and all the windows were open. She could hear birds singing in the garden.

I'll finish everything before my mother comes home from work. She will bring food for dinner, but she will be tired. So I will cook. Maybe after dinner, we can sit outside.

Elspeth was a university student. She was studying history. She lived in a student dormitory near her university. But now it was summer vacation, and she was at home with her mother.

Her home was in a small town, and Elspeth could not find a part-time job anywhere. Her mother worked in the post office. Elspeth worried because they did not have a lot of money. So she tried to help her mother. She cleaned and cooked.

Elspeth was cleaning the kitchen floor when she heard someone knocking at the front door. She went to the door and opened it.

A man was standing on the steps. He was fat, and his face was red and sweaty. He was wearing a suit and tie, and there was a suitcase on the steps next to his feet.

"Can I help you?" asked Elspeth.

The man didn't answer her. He pushed Elspeth away and stepped into the house. He shut the door and said, "You must be Elspeth. You can bring my bag in later. Where is your mother?"

"You can't come into our house! Who are you?" Elspeth wasn't frightened. She was angry.

The man walked into the living room, and then into the kitchen. He looked around. "Where is your mother?" he asked again.

"I'm going to call the police!" Elspeth shouted. She ran to the kitchen table to pick up her phone, but the man was too quick. He picked up her phone and put it in his pocket.

"Your mother isn't here," said the man. "That's OK. Make me some lunch, and bring me some beer. I walked from the bus stop and I'm hot and thirsty."

I can run faster than him, thought Elspeth. *I'll go outside and I will run very quickly to the neighbour's house.*

The man seemed to understand her thoughts.

"Don't think about leaving this house. Don't think about talking to anyone. Your mother will be in a lot of trouble if you do. The police will come and take her away."

"My mother never does anything wrong!" Elspeth shouted.

The man smiled. "Why don't you wait, and ask your mother when she comes home? Ask your mother if she wants to call the police. I am sure she will say 'no'."

Elspeth believed him. *This horrible man can make trouble for my mother,* she thought.

She felt very weak and tired. "We don't have any beer, but I can make you a cheese sandwich and a cup of tea."

"I'll sit in the living room. Bring my food to me."

Elspeth was like a robot. She made a cheese sandwich. She made a cup of tea and filled a glass with water. She took the lunch into the living room and put it on the table in front of the sofa.

The man ate and drank. Elspeth stood by the door watching him. *He smells bad. I don't think he has washed for a long time,* she thought. She felt sick. *He is like a pig. What can he do to hurt my mother?*

The man finished eating. "Bring me some more food," he said. "And then sit in here with me so I can watch you."

When Elspeth brought another sandwich, the television was on.

He pointed to a chair. "Sit," he said.

Elspeth sat down. *What is wrong with me? I feel like a butterfly in a spider's web.*

Time passed very slowly. The man watched the television. Elspeth sat and waited. She could see the time on the television. *My mother will be home soon. She finishes work at 3:30pm today.*

CHAPTER TWO

Elspeth heard her mother's car coming towards the house. She jumped up to go to the door.

"Stop!" said the man.

"No!" Elspeth felt stronger because her mother was coming. When she ran across the living room, the man put his foot out. She fell over his foot onto the floor. When she got up, she saw he was holding a gun.

"Stay!"

"Elspeth! Where are you?" Her mother was coming into the house. "I bought chicken for dinner and we can have a salad from the garden."

Oh, no! thought Elspeth. *I have to stop her!*

"Go back! Go back!" she shouted. But she was too late.

Her mother was still talking as she walked into the living room carrying bags from the supermarket. "We were so busy at work…."

Then her mother saw the man. He was lying on the sofa. Elspeth couldn't see his gun.

"You!" shouted her mother. She dropped the bags of food on the floor.

"Hi, Iris," said the man. "Are you pleased to see me?"

Elspeth's mother's face was white. She was shaking. She was looking at the man.

"Why are you here? What do you want?" she said quietly.

He didn't answer her questions.

"Are you pleased to see me?" he asked again.

"No, no! I didn't want to see you again."

Elspeth wanted to go to her mother. She wanted to put her arms around her. But she was too scared.

Maybe he will take the gun out again. Maybe he will shoot my mother. She knows him. But who is he?

The man laughed. It was not a nice laugh. "So this is a wonderful surprise for you!"

Elspeth's mother fell to the floor. "Get her some water," said the man. "My wonderful surprise was too much for her."

Elspeth ran to the kitchen and came back with a glass of water. "Put her in that chair," said the man pointing to an armchair. Elspeth helped her mother to stand up and sit in an armchair. She gave her mother the water. Her mother drank thirstily. She didn't stop looking at the man.

Elspeth had an idea. *My mother's bag is on the floor with the supermarket bags. If I can get her phone from her bag, I can call for help.*

"I guess you will want dinner," she said. "I'll take the food to the kitchen."

She didn't wait for an answer. She picked up the supermarket bags and her mother's bag from the floor. She walked towards the kitchen.

"Oh no you don't! Do you think I'm stupid? Take the food, but leave the bag. Iris is here with me, and she will die if you try to escape." He put his hand on the pocket of his jacket. *His gun is in that pocket,* thought Elspeth.

Elspeth took the food to the kitchen and put it in the refrigerator. The man was talking to her mother. But he was talking quietly, and she could not hear his words.

When she went back to the living room, her mother said, "We have a house guest." She pointed to the man. "He is staying with us."

Elspeth could not believe it. "No!" she shouted. "Get out of my mother's house. Go! Now!"

The man laughed. "Your mother's house? This is my house, and I will stay here."

Elspeth sat down in a chair next to her mother and took her hand. Her mother's hand was very cold.

"Please, Elspeth," her mother said. "Don't make trouble."

"What do you want me to do?" Elspeth asked her mother, but the man answered.

"I want a good dinner, and something to drink. You have no beer, but find something else."

"We have some wine we use for cooking, and some whisky. Elspeth will find something for you to drink," Elspeth's mother said in a quiet, sad voice.

Elspeth went to the kitchen and found some cooking wine. She poured a glass and took it out to the living room. She put it on the table in front of the sofa. The man took the glass and drank. "Do you want to poison me?" he shouted.

He threw the wine glass. It hit the wall and broke.

Elspeth sat down next to her mother. *Who is this man? He knows my mother. My mother is frightened of him. He says he owns this house. I thought it was my mother's house. He knew my name. My mother always said my father died before I was born. Is he my father? I can't believe it!*

They all heard the sound of a van driving up to the house.

The man jumped up. "Who's that? Who's coming here?"

Elspeth stood up and went over to the window. "It's the courier," she said. "I guess the courier is bringing the study books I ordered for next year at university."

The man took his gun out of his pocket. Elspeth's mother saw it. "Oh no! Cecil! What are you doing?"

"Go to the door," he said to Elspeth. "Be nice to the courier. Do not do anything stupid or I will kill your mother."

The man's name is Cecil. Who is he? What is happening?

Elspeth's legs were shaking. She waited until she heard a knock on the door.

She opened the door. A young man in a red and yellow uniform was standing outside. He was holding a box. It was Ravi! Ravi was a student at Elspeth's university. She liked him very much. He was very handsome and very clever.

Ravi has a summer job with the courier company, she thought.

Ravi smiled. "Hi!"

Oh no! Ravi. Please, please, don't say anything! Elspeth put her finger against her lips.

Ravi was very surprised. *Maybe Elspeth doesn't like me. Maybe her family doesn't want her to know me,* he thought.

"I have a courier parcel for you," he said. "Will you sign for it please?"

He gave Elspeth a clipboard and a pen. But Elspeth did not write her name. She wrote ---*Help! Gun!*---

She gave the clipboard back to Ravi. He read the words. He looked at Elspeth's white face.

"Thank you," he said. "Have a nice evening."

"Thank you," said Elspeth. "I hope you have a nice evening too."

Ravi gave Elspeth the box of books. He got into the courier van and drove away.

When Ravi was back on the street, he stopped the van and took out his phone.

He dialled 111. "What emergency service do you require?" asked the woman on the phone.

"Police," said Ravi. Very soon, another voice was speaking. "Police emergency services. Please give your name and location."

"Uh, Ravi Khan. I am in West Road in Binton."

"Thank you," said the voice. The person sounded very kind and helpful. "What is your problem?"

"I think the girl who lives at one four eight West Road is in trouble."

"What kind of trouble?"

"I am a courier driver. I delivered a parcel there. I asked her to sign for the parcel, but she didn't write her name. She wrote 'Help! Gun!' Something is wrong!"

"Did you see any trouble?"

"No. Everything seemed quiet and normal," answered Ravi.

"Maybe it was a joke."

"No! No!" shouted Ravi. "She is not that kind of girl!"

The kind voice suddenly sounded very cold. "Do you know her?"

"Yes. We go to the same university. She is a very nice person!"

"Mr Khan. You are wasting our time. We have many people with real problems. I think you are playing a joke on us. If you call again, you will be in big trouble."

"But..!" shouted Ravi. He was too late. The other person ended the phone call.

Ravi drove back to the courier company. His boss was angry. "Why did you take so long? We have many more parcels to deliver."

Ravi told his boss about Elspeth's message. His boss laughed. "Many people play jokes on courier drivers. They think it is funny. You know this girl. So she wants to play a joke on you. Maybe she wants a date. Forget it!"

I don't know what to do, thought Ravi. *Was Elspeth playing a joke on me?*

He filled his van with boxes and went out to take them to houses all over the town.

CHAPTER THREE

After Ravi drove away, Elspeth went back into the living room. She put the box of books on the floor.

Her mother was sitting in an armchair looking at Cecil.

My mother looks very small. She looks very old, thought Elspeth *Who is Cecil? He is a very bad man.*

"You go to university," he said. "You think you are very clever. But I am smarter than you. Do everything I tell you, or bad things will happen to your mother. Bring me whisky! Now!"

Elspeth looked at her mother. "Please, Elspeth. Do it," her mother said quietly.

The whisky was in a low cupboard. Elspeth found it and took the bottle and a glass to the living room. Cecil poured a glass of whisky and drank it very quickly.

"You," he said, pointing at Elspeth. "Go and make me a good meal."

Elspeth went to the kitchen.

Did Ravi understand my message? Will he go to the police? Why is my mother so scared of this man?

Her head was hurting. She looked out of the window. In summer, the days are long, and it was bright and sunny. The birds were singing. She looked at the vegetable garden, and she had an idea.

She went back into the living room and said, "Do you want vegetables or salad?"

"Vegetables! I want meat and potatoes and something sweet."

"The potatoes are in a sack in the garden shed."

Cecil pointed his gun at Elspeth's mother. "Stand up, Iris."

It took Iris a long time to stand up. Cecil put his arm around her shoulders. He pushed Iris into the kitchen. Elspeth followed them.

He looked at Elspeth. "Go to the garden shed and get the potatoes. I will watch you from the window. If you try to escape, your mother will die. Is there rope in the shed?"

"No!" said Elspeth.

"Yes," said her mother.

"Bring the potatoes and the rope. I am watching you."

Elspeth went out of the house. She walked slowly to the shed. The garden was so pretty. There were many flowers. The tomatoes were big and red. The lettuces were ready to eat. But everything was wrong. Cecil was watching her. He had a gun, and Elspeth did not know what to do.

Elspeth walked into the shed and the door shut behind her. But there was a window at the end of the shed, so she could see well. Elspeth saw the BBQ. The cover was red. *Where is the spray paint? I have to be quick!* She pulled the cover off the BBQ and found some spray paint.

She used the spray paint to write ---*HELP*--- on the cover. She opened the window and threw the cover on the ground.

I have to hurry, or he will kill my mother. Elspeth filled a bag with potatoes and found the rope. *I hate this, but I must save my mother.*

She hurried back into the house. She put the bag of potatoes on the counter and turned to Cecil.

"Here is the rope."

"Bring the rope and that chair." He pointed to a kitchen chair.

He pushed Elspeth's mother back into the living room. Elspeth followed them.

"Put the chair here," Cecil pointed to a place in front of the sofa. Then he pushed her mother onto the chair. She was so weak, she fell off the chair.

"Pick her up," said Cecil. "Use the rope and tie her to the chair."

Elspeth looked at her mother. "I can't do this," she said.

"Do it," said her mother. Then she said very quietly, "I want you to live."

Elspeth cried while she tied her mother to the chair.

Cecil got up and checked the ropes.

"OK," he said. "Now go to the kitchen and cook."

Elspeth thought hard while she was cooking. *The police have not come. Maybe Ravi didn't understand. Maybe he didn't call the police. I must save my mother. I must do something.*

She was peeling the potatoes when she had an idea. She looked at the small sharp knife she was using. *He is drinking a lot of whisky. Maybe he will get drunk and fall asleep. Then maybe I will have a chance to attack him. Where can I hide the knife?* Elspeth was wearing socks. She pushed the knife down the side of her sock. She felt better.

CHAPTER FOUR

Cecil ate all the food Elspeth cooked. "Something sweet," he shouted. "Go and get me something sweet!"

Elspeth gave him ice cream and cookies. She looked at the whisky bottle. It was almost empty. *Please fall asleep!* she thought.

Cecil finished eating and picked up the gun. He pointed the gun at Elspeth. "Come with me. I am going to find somewhere to lock you and your mother up, so I can have a good sleep."

Outside the back door of the house was a small room with a washing machine.

"This is a good place," he said. He pushed Elspeth back to the living room and said, "Untie your mother!" Her mother fell on the floor. Elspeth tried to pick her up.

"Leave her. Take this chair and another chair from the kitchen to that small room. Remember, your mother will die if you don't do it." Cecil carried her mother and followed her.

In the laundry room he said, "Tie your mother to the chair!" Then, he tied Elspeth to the other chair.

Oh no! He will find the knife! thought Elspeth. But Elspeth was lucky. Cecil didn't find the knife. The ropes were tight. They hurt Elspeth's arms and legs.

He found towels and tied them around their mouths so they couldn't speak.

Then he went out. Elspeth looked at her mother's eyes. They were wide and scared. Elspeth was very angry.

She looked at the window. It was almost dark. *I don't know what time it is. But when it is very dark, he will be sleeping. Then I must try to get the knife.*

CHAPTER FIVE

Ravi was very worried. He worked until 7:00 pm. Every day, when he finished working, he parked his van outside the courier office. He locked it, and took the key to the boss's office. There was a row of hooks for keys.

Today, Ravi did something different. When he went into the office, his boss was not there. Ravi did not put the key to the van on the hook. He put it in his pocket. Then he went outside, got on his bicycle and rode away.

If my boss discovers I have the key to the van, I will lose my job. But I don't care. Later, when there is no one at the courier office, I will take the van. I will drive to Elspeth's house. I want to know if she is OK.

When it was very dark outside, Elspeth started to move her chair. Finally, she moved it enough, and it fell over. She hit the floor hard. It hurt a lot. *I hope Cecil didn't hear the noise,* she thought. Then Elspeth tried very hard, but she could not get the knife in her sock. She looked at her mother.

Her mother was looking at the door. Then Elspeth heard a sound at the door. Someone was trying to open it!

Suddenly, Ravi came into the room. He was using the light from his smartphone. He was very surprised.

He saw an older woman tied to a chair with a towel around her mouth. "What!" he shouted. He ran to Elspeth's mother and took the towel from her mouth. "Are you OK?" he asked.

"Please be quiet!" said Elspeth's mother. "There is a very dangerous man in the house."

Ravi was trying to untie the ropes. "I'll turn the light on so I can see."

"No! No! He might see the light!" Elspeth's mother was very scared.

Then Ravi saw Elspeth lying on the floor. She was still tied to her chair. He took the towel from Elspeth's face.

"Are the police coming?" asked Elspeth quietly.

"No. I'm sorry. I called the police," said Ravi. "They laughed at me. They said people were always playing jokes on courier delivery drivers. So I went back to the depot and I told my boss. I said, 'I know her. We go to the same university'.

"He laughed at me too. He said, 'Maybe she likes you. Maybe she wrote ---Help! Gun!--- because she wants you to take her out on a date. Don't worry about it. I have more parcels for you to deliver.'

"I worked late, but I was worried. When I finished, I came back here. It is dark outside. I can't see lights in the house. When I walked to the back of the house, I fell over the BBQ cover. I used the light from my phone and I saw your message. Then I heard a sound from this little room. So I came here."

Ravi lifted Elspeth and the chair up.

"I have a knife in my sock," said Elspeth softly. "You can cut the ropes."

"No!" said her mother quietly. "First, please do something for me. I don't know you, but I think you are kind and brave. Please go to the house. Maybe you can see if the man in the house is sleeping. Please be very careful. If it is safe, we can escape."

"OK," said Ravi. "But I'm going to call the police first."

"No! Please! Go quickly."

Ravi went outside and closed the door.

CHAPTER SIX

After Ravi went away, Elspeth asked her mother. "Who is Cecil?"

"He is your uncle," she said sadly. "He is my brother. He is a very bad man, but when he was a little boy, I loved him very much.

"When he was older, he did many bad things. When he was about twenty years old, he disappeared. For a long time I didn't know where he was, or what he was doing.

"I was twenty-five years old when I met your father. He was a policeman. We got married. We were very happy. But a few weeks after you were born, your father was trying to stop a bank robbery. One of the bank robbers killed him.

"Then, Cecil came back. He said, 'You can live in this house for free.' He often stole things and he wanted somewhere to hide them, until he could sell them. I knew it was wrong, but he was my little brother. You were a tiny baby, and I had no money. So I helped him. No one knew. Then, one night, when you were two years old, he came here. He said, 'I tried to steal money from a bank. The police are looking for me. I'm going to run away. I'm going to go to another country.'

"He took all the money I had in the house. He took your father's watch, and everything else he could find to sell. When he was leaving, he said, 'You can't tell anyone about me. You have been helping me. The police will put you in prison and take Elspeth away.' And then…
And then…"

Elspeth's mother was crying so hard she couldn't speak.

"It's OK," said Elspeth. "You can tell me after we escape."

They heard a noise outside the door. Elspeth and Iris were so scared, they couldn't breathe.

Someone came into the room. It was Ravi!

"I think it's OK," he said quietly. "I went into your house. I heard someone snoring loudly. I am sure he is asleep."

Ravi took the knife from Elspeth's sock. He cut the ropes.

Elspeth and Ravi helped her mother. Very quietly, they walked out of the room, into the garden and into the road.

"How did you come here?" asked Elspeth.

"I took a van from the courier company. I parked about one hundred metres from here," said Ravi.

They walked to the courier van. They helped Iris climb into the van. Then Ravi called the police.

"Please come to one four eight West Road. A man attacked two women. They are safe now, but he is in the house with a gun."

"Who are you? Where are you?" asked the woman at the police station.

"I am Ravi Khan. We will wait at the end of West Road. You will find us there."

Ravi drove the van down West Road. He parked at the corner. Iris, Elspeth and Ravi sat in the van and waited. They didn't talk.

I took the courier van, thought Ravi. *I will lose my job and maybe I will go to prison. But it's OK. I know I did the right thing.*

Soon, they saw police cars. The cars went down West Road and stopped outside the house. Then a black van passed them. After about 20 minutes, an ambulance with flashing lights and a loud siren raced down the road.

CHAPTER SEVEN

Finally, the police cars came back. A car stopped next to the van. Ravi opened the window. A policeman walked to the door of the van.

"Are you Ravi Khan?"

"Yes, I'm Ravi Khan. Did you find the man with the gun?"

"We found the man with the gun. We are very happy. We have been looking for him. But you must come to the police station."

"My mother is so tired. It has been very difficult for her," said Elspeth.

"I'm sorry. But you must come. We want to hear your story."

Ravi drove to the police station. A police car followed them. Elspeth was very surprised when her mother said, "I'm so sorry. Everything is my fault. The police will know my story. They will put me in prison because I helped Cecil. You will be alone."

"Elspeth will not be alone," said Ravi. "I will look after her. My mother will look after her. Please don't worry. Maybe the police will not be interested in what you did so many years ago."

At the police station, the police took them to three different rooms.

A nice policewoman asked Elspeth many questions. Elspeth told her everything.

"Did you know the man who came to the house?" asked the policewoman.

"No. I didn't know him."

"Why did he come to your house?"

"I don't know," said Elspeth.

Elspeth didn't tell the policewoman that the man with the gun was her uncle. She didn't say anything about her mother's story.

The policewoman gave Elspeth a cup of tea. "Please wait," she said.

"My mother! I want to see my mother."

The policewoman smiled. "You can see her soon."

She went out of the room, and Elspeth was alone.

After a long time, the policewoman came back. "Your mother wants to go home. But I am sorry. It is a crime scene, and you can't go there now. But a police car will take you to a hotel. Come with me."

There was a police car waiting outside. Elspeth's mother was sitting in the back of the police car. The policewoman came with them.

The car drove to a hotel. It was 3:00am when Elspeth and her mother went to a nice double room.

"You had a bad time," said the policewoman. "I will leave you now. I hope you can sleep. Maybe tomorrow, or the day after tomorrow, you can go home."

She went to the door. Then she stopped. She smiled at Elspeth. "The young man who helped you likes you very much. If he asks you for a date, please say 'yes'."

She went away. For the first time, Elspeth looked at her mother. She was surprised. Her mother was relaxed. She looked strong.

"Are you OK?" said Elspeth.

"Yes. I am very good."

"Do the police know you helped Cecil? Are you in trouble with the police?"

"No. They are very nice. I said, "Cecil was my brother. It was his house. I didn't see him for seventeen years. I was frightened of him. They said, 'Don't worry anymore. When we went to your house, Cecil woke up. He fired his gun. So we fired our guns at him. He is dead.'"

"Do the police know you helped Cecil?" asked Elspeth.

"No. Only Cecil knew I helped him. And now he is dead. I am safe."

"Are you sad?" asked Elspeth. "He was your brother."

"No!" shouted Iris. "I am happy! I didn't tell you the rest of my story. It was too difficult. But I will tell you now.

"Seventeen years ago, when Cecil planned to go to another country, he took everything he could sell from the house. The last thing he said to me was, 'Your husband died, trying to stop a bank robbery. I was part of that gang. I killed your husband'. He laughed."

"I understand," said Elspeth. "Let's go to bed."

THANK YOU

Thank you for reading Elspeth and the Visitor. (Word count: 4,861) We hope you enjoyed it.

There are quizzes about this book on our free study site I Talk You Talk Press EXTRA. http://italk-youtalk.com

If you would like to read more graded readers, please visit our website http://www.italkyoutalk.com

Other Level 2 graded readers include
Adventure in Rome
Andre's Dream
A Passion for Music
Christmas Tales
Danger in Seattle
Don't Come Back
Dressed for Success
Finders Keepers…
Hunted in Hong Kong
John Sees a Murder
Marcy's Bakery
Men's Konkatsu Tales
Message in a Bottle
Murder in Marrakech
Murder on Whale Island

Salaryman Secrets!
Stories for Halloween
The Cruise Ship
The Perfect Wedding
The House in the Forest
The Kindness of Strangers
The School on Bolt Street
Train Travel
Trouble in Paris
Who's There?
Women's Konkatsu Tales

ABOUT THE AUTHOR

I Talk You Talk Press is an award-winning Japan-based publisher of language textbooks, graded readers and language learning/teaching resources.

Our team is made up of highly experienced language teachers and translators, who have all studied at least one additional language to an advanced level.

This experience enables us to design our materials from the perspective of both the teacher and the learner. We consult with both teachers and language learners when designing our textbooks and graded readers, and test our materials extensively in the classroom before publication.

We are a fast-growing press, and currently publish graded readers for learners of English. We publish new graded readers monthly.

www.ingramcontent.com/pod-product-compliance
Lightning Source LLC
LaVergne TN
LVHW051517170726
843492LV00002B/978